W9-ADX-975

Rochelle Owens

SHEMUEL

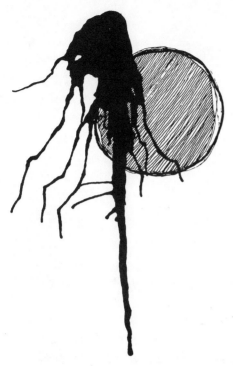

Rochelle Owens

SHEMUEL

MIDDLEBURY COLLEGE LIBRARY

with drawings by
Gaylord Schanilec

New Rivers Press

1979

PS
3565
W57
S54

Copyright © 1979 by Rochelle Owens
Library of Congress Catalog Number: 79-64149
ISBN 0-89823-006-3
All rights reserved
Book Design: C. W. Truesdale
Typesetting: John Minczeski
Photograph of the author: Pat Hill

Grateful acknowledgement is made to the following publications where some of these poems first appeared: *Diana's Bimonthly*, *Poetry Now*, and *Kosmos*.

Shemuel has been published with the aid of generous supporting grants from the National Endowment for the Arts and the New York State Council on the Arts.

New Rivers Press books are distributed by
    SBD: Small Press Distribution
    Jeanetta Jones Miller
    1636 Grand View Avenue
    Kensington, California
    94707

Shemuel has been manufactured in the United States of America for New Rivers Press (C. W. Truesdale, Editor/Publisher), 1602 Selby Avenue, St. Paul, Minnesota 55104 in a first edition of 1000 copies of which 25 have been signed and numbered by the author and the artist.

This book is for George

Imagination is generator of the word as act/event. In *Shemuel* the journey begun in *The Joe 82 Creation Poems* (Black Sparrow) and *The Joe Chronicles*, Part 2, continues to explore through patterns of force the conjunction of the old and the new, the spiritual and the physical.

I

THE MASTER MECHANIC

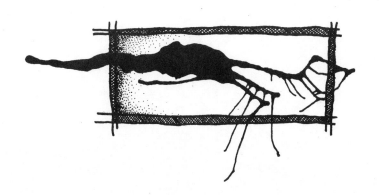

BAROQUE BLISTER SONG

let me eye You

whistling　　　during　　　an evil hour

the dying fish

is the clearest Meaning

the Black

Savage Burning moving 1

Square

suffocation

on

the worlde's Surface

the　　Mind

of the　　　　blood.

ELIOT'S BLISTER SONG

old brain
Selah   the levels
of The Enfolding
& then what
cuts back?
what does it mean
this technological
blood-sticky rain

I See the Angel Gabriel
give
solace

the Meaning cleanses
the violence
to
birds

MILTON'S BLISTER SONG

What is the color of

the flowing Worlde

death-dove

a forest of Ripening
death

apples
breast-rib

earth unites water

the Bangkok cats piss

all grass is the same   the
jackals blacker than

a gasp

4

tiny oranges cells bright split
like chalk the legs of workers
horse-fly the memorable vulgar
sunset now we face our acid test
                              exile
point out that 220 million see
visions 10 million see drought
this country huddles beneath
bananna trees kerosene and cement
                              bleakest
nepotism colossal 13 million
sharp blows then four million
from bangladesh then the war
aging us all alike very vitals
                              destroyed

        the air force the

left wing

     moving the colonels all

crazier than the generals the

truckmen

       sucking pipe bombs

Joe's fault

     Joe's Fault

        joe's pro-

blem he declared his own people

    crazier than Congress so

the distrubances we trust fully

before they explode around us we

trust the minister who eats tran

quilizers & zips up his fly with

our family & attorney watching

     the Act

6

mr sincerity loves country music
that i didn't dream about in the
sunshade faces woken up damn fid
dler watch out brother 50 years
ago a nightrider can see clearly
the childhood of oppression doub
led war song in repose Uncle Unc
le in agony for catholic men jus
t jammed together anti-semitic q
ueen of sheba finding out she's
plain broke buying used camels &
dried figs flaking off flecks of
salt cod the source of the drago
n of the sinai blue denim large
golden nose-ring our baby from t
he land of hittites my former se
lf itching to get even & then we
t

J. S. BACH'S BLISTERS

blood   of the   savage

          the nose-ring is loved

by the catholics of rome

                       whistling

     & eyeing

           the surface of

     the negev the jews technological

angel gabriel levels breast-rib

                 black apple

       what is the color

         of a gasp

8

listen to
rollo may
for fear
of cleopa
tra pushi
ng the we
alth of s
udanese s
hits the
farmer kn
ows the p
rice of c
amels & t
ired & an
gry just
picks the
most fant
astic bar
gain & ea
ts his oy
l & olive

why can't i have the shicksa
wailed the queen of sheba why
must it be the descendent of
haille sellasie & the original queen

my existence is not forever so
why can't i have the foreign
woman from across the eber why
water unites earth the limit
is boldness so why can't i have

the strange woman thousands &
thousands all grass is the same
jackals let loose their knees
the adventure turns us white
the foreign stranger's breast near

my own the perfection of the
dream receives ripening apples

i deserve even more of a medal
than ezekiel for keeping the f
aith the day of this human rac
e & floor wax
        the meaning of ter
rible hiding according to all
the compassion the honor of th
e nations is
        skull song cracked
truth the rice flesh is skull
song jeroboam in the land of
egypt & the nest
        of   spoilers   t
he annihilation walking & jud
ah only hallowing & shining t
hru the queen's memory amen d
aughter of his perfection of

     dream

it wasn't my fault the drought
it's $40 a year
my rising voice of corruption
i am a moved go
dddddeeesssss i wore wool pais
ley saris with
a vest of idealism my brother
is an autoerot
icist living in france now we
are a nation o
f many famous races everywher
e i would like
a new museum built there is a
drought that i
never would have wanted if i
could have hel
ped it kerosene & cement shor
tages exaspera
te me

12

my fallen shrine is
woolworths they have
retired it's presiden
t

what now in multi-to
ne do you expect to g
ather anywhere the num
b
er of deaths is bent
on hell without succe
ss last week only hour
s

to go the jury inter
viewed the task force
because of tape worms t
h
e men were not relieve
ed

the politicians like good
wardrobes a goldfish with
fire in his eye one of the
nice things is the boast
of a leader he says i am
38 years old & i know what
pakistan feels like i could
touch the genitals of the
new baby country forever
what do you want from me
mother teresa of albania
she's well-publicized like

tom flanagan from the uni
versity of california who
reflects the silver minnow
in his naked rib-cage

14

night work that night there
were several strikes 13 dollars
the pregnant woman of ireland

stole who was a cleaning woman
mother of four children the
numbing one was in the jail-

house & resented the health
& bad history in the working-
class district on end for years

many outside the buildings cried
for the sickness in the government
building i found two children

huddling together in the cold
night her own child has no family
her toes are gnarled vaguely she talks

outside

              many

                         who were stolen

  of 13 dollars

                   outside the bad history

of sickness the night work

                    & the gnarled

           toes dig

                 into the eyes

     of irish jack the prize

fighter of finally no reasons

                       very blue eyes

          she scrubs toilets
     her anxiety ringing

                 she's trying to
     get more drinks down her

cleaners union
he hit her in
the churning
body the room
smells of americans
they verily say

in cooperation
with the cooperation
of the union of
civic automobiles
we wish to stunt
the growth of

your gentle unborn
children so that
the government of
cyprus will know
a pub from a hole
in the ground.

THE DANCE OF THE BRACELETS

queen shemuel
investigated the prophets
she pulled punches with prophets
bored into the horny side of prophets

queen shemuel
played ball with the prophets studied
the phenomena of propane gas
a world of illusions
the dizzy prophets the Voice

of something
queen shemuel uttered words of praise
for the prophets
who dazed the whole of america
who sucked the eyes
out of the sockets

18

the sweeper is poor payed
the corruption is making a
speech
the scandler is payed
poor
the diaspora man named
eleazor katz is poor payed
he kept his coat on
when he prayed
the plan is
to slow down
the poor payed ones

to work like the chinese
across the river eber
henry garcia established
blood mixing with the children of ur

lower lips scandaling
the judges of the community like pigs
with jewels in their snouts
the sophisticated leaders
fewer than 10,000 assessed by municipal

officials during the terrible
wave of heat from across the
river declared a class of
negroes any negroe sitting there
a king

i would like a sports car
to nestle in said queen s
hemuel the pipik of a man
from gaza to sport fish w
ith dogs cats a cat named
mehmedbasich giving relie
f's blessing enough to su
pport a life-time i insis
t that trucks contain 20
tons of prepared beef from
the land of the medes & s
lippers of a sturdy mater
ial that will not rot in
the desert something that
really works for a change

yes the uproar in memphis
was a limitation stemming from
monday night   yes & yes
                    when mr. kim renewed his
quantitative improvements & sprinkled
travelers with 100 year dragon's balls
          yes when mr. chin in chengtu
laughed & with an astro chart strongly
recommended & surprisingly shifted the
embrace of his new perspective
                    yes & yes
& he found that the unruly youth
      dedicated himself to frequent thievery
          yes & yes   in szechwan

22

there is no right control
there is only duke elling
ton & his orchestra there
is no leftist cultural re
volution there are only s
ocial leaders & the selec
tion of rooms & the hong
kong credentials of the n
o. 1 man particularly the
commissar in szechwan & i
n chengtu & in memphis &
in belfast & in the land
of haman the evil for 10
dollars a night you can s
ee them all in a comforta
ble bathroom with a telep
hone & electric fan

he hit her in the churning
body   she hit him in the worried
                              body
                he hadn't earned a nickle in
        a week   why should she take
        the loafer's shit
                        in belfast she hit
                him in the churning stomack
        in dublin he hit her in the
                              pregnant
body
                it has become a way of life
        he a strongman hitting she a
        strongwoman hitting
        they tell the medes you don't understand
                our ways

the soldier
& the sailor
& the crator
& the muddy
rocks & the
monsoon rain
& the large
house without
a garden of
onions let
alone a cucumber
through the
deserted village
you can hear
the unborn cucumbers
& onions crying
the sobs say again
& again everything
o everything is gone.

certainly the united states
is guilty
worldwide contraction
pressure of 40 billion dollars
paralyzing & pushing at interest-rate
differentials
persuasion
paralyzing european & japanese hands
the bubble will burst
on guilty aunt dora &
fish marengo
will smoothly push
the suspicious
questions out of the weaker
countries of the globe
play fast & loose
innocent people's lives
are in our dominion

II

OBLIVION SKEIN

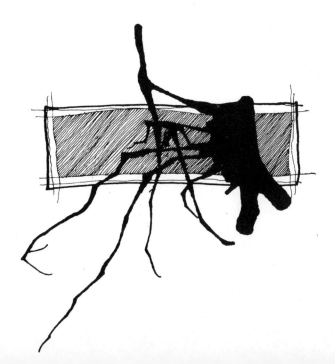

who is the yawner
of uz   does his quiet
                    expose soon
grey rot   catching swells with
nothing
            who is the madwoman beyond
            the weeds
                        weaving with thunder
in snaps oblivion in fingers more
ruthless
            than a wink from queen
            shemuel
                        from queen shemuel
her fingers snap up mathematical
space

the back shadow idol
in the back alley of uz

you of the back alley your
shadow idol is in back of you

you of backs & shadow idols in
the back alley of fetid uz

uz is a stinking fetid alley you
follow the shadows of your idols

your idols shadow you in uz &
everywhere you are in the back

uz shadows you uz makes you forever
fetid the back alley of shadows follow

you are fetid follow fetidness your
back alleys stink & everywhere you

are in the alley of backness uz will
not save you your idols shadow you

across the river

no-feathered

birds missing primary & secondary feathers

swollen feet

abandoned pesticide horrible residue

obviously

polychlorinated biphenyls

world's oceans

obviously   breakdown   obviously   breakdown

hate health

the great gulls

sewage   obviously   midway

between weekend visits

is of significance

obviously

hate god

hate god

make more breakdown

obviously

more breakdown is good
breakdown breakdown is
good breakdown more is
alright o.k. joe joe i
t's o.k. g.i. remember
chocolate bar is o.k.
more breakdown is good
great breakdown is o.k.
more is good breakdown
remember g.i. joe is o.
k. more breakdown is go
od breakdown breakdown
is good breakdown more
is alright o.k. joe joe
it's o.k. g.i. remember
chocolate bar is o.k. m
ore breakdown is good m
ore breakdown is irregular

we are coming to america
set your chin not too fa
r from the lord one that
is to come is samael wi
th hairs causing thy str
ength to turn the coal f
ires to frustration why
should ye seek the sin t
o make israel sin i disc
lose it to thee it is we
ll that you laugh accord
ing to the rules of the
pentagon exterminate the
abominations of the inha
bitants of tyre the fire
of tyre the transgressio
ns of the city of gaza &
the city of ashkelon & t
he city of edom & the ci
ty of jerusalem & woe &
woe & joe's joe's city

everything's repellent
                    i find it in
                    violence. velvet
dusk time past june
        a ritual to enfold nah nah
                        sightless dogs
say nah nah like the beggars of uz say
                    no no no nay
it's fascinating the knee of baal is always
                    in place & the
promiscuous egyptians watch a man make his
                    voice sound like
glockenspiels dusk time past june
        pathos is the same absurd
                        in the land of uz

he hit her in
the rocking b
ody she hit h
im in the wat
ching face sh
e gave him a bi
rthday party
he hit her in
the mike she
hit him in th
e temple he h
it her in the
flag she hit
his fag he hi
t her mother
she laughed h
e watched her
really get go
ing she hit h
im in the voi
ce fogbound

she gave him a camera
he gave her an afternoon opera
she wrote down the words
of the fisherman of gaza

he thought of the fogbound
grin
she wondered about
agony he moved 20 pounds of
complicated neutrality
she danced in a
minor dance group in uz
he liked the extraordinary lighting of
uz
she slightly shifted her reasons
for liking uz
he pondered on her churning
body she hit him in the child sound

ESSAY

thus it is not surprising
thus the morality thus is
contagious thus we allow
socks scarce tho they are
thus we allow them thus
we use straw in infinite
space over it all thus
we pop the weightless

buttons of our overcoats
thus energize ourselves
with scarce cheese thus
the effort to understand
is impeccable on top of
that there is no underst
anding for example make
clear the face of people

make clear the face
is changed to faces
make clear the faces
which ear is slept on
which thus is imprisoned
thus because in ruzyne
we ate goat meat & allowed
intercourse with mr. yin

we understand the energized
condition of wives of former
impeccable strawed men thus
clear the fact up for mr. yen
who with his wife scarce knew
the clear ringing freedom bell
in the village of gaza or thus
spelled his own space copping out

we allow ourselves
to cop out thus po
wer is impeccable
the measure of thu
s those acts in ou
r own sweet time
asserted but in ruz
yne the fatigue tha
t the crime permitt
ed we were in no hu
rry to gather the w
ool from the sheep
in babylon or in mem
phis or in uz or in
gaza or in pittsburg
or in flatbush or in
los angeles or in joe's
city

queen shemuel said to thee

the angel of death accosts

man strange gods kill him

the wicked

watcheth with a bad

melody functioning from his

anus

who can know what stinks

in gad?

satan & yezer & angel

of death are one

the anus functions with a bad melody

the wicked watcheth

with a bad strange god

standing near

who can watch with a
bad strange god stan
ding near who can ho
ld back the song fro
m the anus the melod
y of the nether worl
d man persuades the
yezer to rule over h
im all are other nam
es that taketh away
the soul the soul th
at sits in joe's cit
y & the shadow of de
ath is not an unconf
irmed report the sma
ll boys see it in th
e kites they fly in
joe's city & seeks t
o slay him is no myt
h

he hit her in

the curling body

she hit him in the

purple heart

he cocked his

wallet at her face

she stuck

her pencil at his

function

she hit him in

the churning body he hit her

in the troubled heart

she hit him

in the velvet balls

he hit her

in the plate-glass

womb

in dublin town

in london the factory
men are obedient to yezer they
churn strong liquor in their
lips
from the moment of his
circumcision a london factory man
ponders on the significance
of the holy ones
what's eating you
sez queen shemuel to the man
who deserted uz-land
who exploits you today
what ponders
holy ones what exploits
capitalists
when mr. yin saw strong liquor
he remembered the
unfashionable intercourse
yestiddy

also he was bringing
back the fat back of
bullocks the backs
were very fat very
very hairy also

also they find they
can live without
the first god also
they find they can
live & do wrongdoing

& not suffer also it
results in their getting
very very rich $51.50
a minute without the
bother of offerings

to the lord

sometimes for a cute
curse the lord makes
the eye stink & this
frightens the shopkeepers
& the growers of grain
                & then to
impair the power of the
first god & inhibit the cute curse
the grain keepers write poems against

          the lord they
squeeze their righteousness hard
into purity & take on even the
          angel of death
        sometimes goodly alternatives
occur out of the whirlwinds of the younger
gods
        in the summer after the holy ones
squeeze their righteousness hard
into purity against the lord

who can know what
they do in gaza or
edom
   in a minute
one can know
     one can know
in a minute if a
woman is fallen
     one can know
in a minute if
a man betrays his
brother
     one can know
in a minute if the
people love the lord

44

became
known
absolving
she hit him
in the corrupt body
became known
fully cursing
he hit her in the
scary eye
absolving
faster than a
whoring son of mr. yin
faster than a
fly eats honey
absolving
within the letter
the spirit of the
law

i put my other report
in the treasure hour
of the lord i witnessed
the nuptials of a
daughter of mr. yin
i watched the bizarre
bathing of her shaded
areas by concubines
i violated the pits
of her toes with my
sheeps tongue
the angel of death
scorned me among
the sons of men
i became campaign
treasurer in gad
the sons of ishmael
tickled my fancy

THE SMELL OF APPLES

by the negev
what is the color of a
gasp   what is the color of
apple   breastrib
black apples or
the nose-rings loved
by the python-lipped sons of
ishmael
sarah's eye
levels
earth has grass & bangkok cats
snake has heat
behind the rusted
jaws
snake sez   whyfore ye die for
judea t'aint all grass the same
besides make yer covenant with me
takes just seconds

the smell of apples
by the negev
the color of a gasp
is the color of apple
the rusted nail
behind black apples
breast-rib &
nose-rings
drool of samael
evil archangel
crippler dabbler in
tin nipples & python
lips of onan &
hysteria of sons
of ishmael
what could be
worse the
snake of course

         he hit her in the
     churning body
              she hit him in
       the knocking body   he hit her
    earth/ she hit him
              behind the breast-rib
  he hit her singing
             mouth
       she snuck up
    behind the nose-rings
               behind the apples/
         she crawled   like snotting
       samael after spewing
     onan   then she hit him thenshehithim
   in the python ventricle/ of his rotting
being   then even the rusted nail
      or the cursing of sarah
    or the scorn of ishmael couldn't
   draw the angel of death near

say make your lousy
covenant or watchamicallit
with me
canaan is the cat's meow
you can bust a gut
on port & apples

even eat snake-meat
or suck a one-eyed tit
of a crazy lady from
sodom
what about grabbing off
something that don't grow

on trees like apples
the balls of an uncircumcised
lad from gad
i could introduce you to
lot's daughters
bring ornaments & wine

let pale hand of
infamous canaanite
lo eighty hands steal
a bony thumb out of
new york door-locks &
let the eighty hands
of canaanites seek a
redemption & let them
kill the evil yezer
that modifys my words
So that the words – Let no gods before me be worshipped –
shift & twist & slant &
alter to – Worship a hundred gods before
me
& tho i bend my knee to
moloch
i am righteous & saved

III

THE PROPHET &
THE STRANGE GOD

yezer is nothing
the strange god
between one part
of the eating heart
the eating heart parts
apple-soul
tooth/technique
yezer is ridicule
of the sage
the bowels of nothing
yezer is nothing
produced
the gas of the
compulsive one
strange god is evil yezer nothing is yezer
but yezer

possible the guerrillas
possible the jurists
possible the gnats
possible the camels
possible the millions of
tons of bombs
possible the front pages
possible the social revolutions
possible the american policies
possible the country's actions
possible the light dawns

on governments
possible the mental testing
possible the facts are unknown
possible the shoddy thinking
possible the little or nothing
possible the taxpayer a scapegoat
& a sheep's ass

moloch
god twist & slant
redemption & let them
steal out of door-locks
joe's city is new york
let pale hand of
infamous canaanite
lo eighty hands steal
your door-locks
a bony thumb twist
your tits
so that you bend your knee
to me & seek me to
whisper a consolation
to thee
but i scorn thee
thou hast made a pact
with a golden goat
&there can be no peace
between us

again i say let
a piss-hued hand of a
hot greedy canaanite
lo eighty stinky hands
steal
with a bony thumb hooking
like a harlot's eye
into your door-lock
& may your enemies
dance a circle dance
& serve milk to the
thieves that slay
your heart
because you listened not
to my voice
may you bend your knee
to a dumb goat
& scream in a jackal's
song
i am saved i am saved

let pale hand of
infamous canaanite
lo eighty hands steal
a bony thumb out of
new york door-locks &
let the eighty hands
of canaanites seek a
redemption & let them
kill the evil yezer
that modifys my words
so that the words let
no gods before me be
worshipped
shift & twist & slant &
alter to
worship a hundred gods
before me & tho
you bend your knee to
moloch thou art righteous
& saved

so yesterday
they yelled
traiganio para fuera!
so we can hang
him from the pipes

we identify him as the
treacherous one
he never fully
explained how
he came to be

one of us/
today in the press
they said i was
against myself
how crazy

the one i'm against
is you & so
i cast my fate
with
myself

queen shemuel said
it comes from the law
it comes from the law
it comes from the law
it comes from the law
it comes from the law

five times

the assumption is enforcement
the assumption is enforcement
the assumption is enforcement
the assumption is enforcement
the assumption is enforcement
seven times

the assumption is enforcement
the assumption is enforcement

now everything's accurate

and be fined
mr. yin said
in mexico city
you were the key
dealer in opium
you killed in
olden china
& now you are
the third alleged
fiend driving
in an automobile
containing in the
trunk 264 pounds
of the effecting
drug/ next you
will want a private
plane to fly you
to the nether world
so you can curb
the flow of the
craving demons of
samael

my vulva is nicer
said miriam
my vulva is nicer said
sheba
my vulva is nicer
said cleopatra
my vulva is nicer said
deborah
my vulva is nicer said
dinah my vulva is
nicer said jemimah
my vulva is nicer
said leah
my vulva is nicer said
the shulamite
my vulva is fatal
said rachel

my vulva is nicer
said sheba
my vulva is nicer
said leah
my vulva is nicer
said dora
my vulva is victorious
said doloris
my vulva is nicer
said cleopatra
my vulva is nicer
said jemimah
my vulva is sweeter
said rita
my vulva is great
said fate
my vulva is fatal
said rachel

i will go in unto her
i will go in unto her
i will go in unto her
i will go in unto her
i will go in unto her
i will go in unto her
i will go in unto her
i will go in unto her
i will go in unto her
i will go in unto her
i will go in unto her
i will go in unto her
i will go in unto her
i will go in unto her
i will go in unto her
i will go in unto her
i will go in unto her

62

shemuel the queen
said ─ ─ go ask
someone else
to fast with you
rest your head
on a great stone/
stone your head
on a great stone/
you did not fast
so stone your head
go to a great stone
rest your head
they will stone you
they will want to/
ask anyone
they will want to
sacrifice you for the sake
of heav'n
& the city joe woe joe's
city

this is joe's city
wretched city cast
your hooked eye the
slanting nose of a
harlot
left none without
a fuck
them on the edge of a
nipple
the edge of a sword
in the land
of mizpah
on the border of
og mr. yin
on the edge of a
nipple
there is rest from
war

shemuel the queen
said — go ask
someone else
to fast with you
rest your head
on the great stone
stone your head
you did not fast
they will stone you
ask anyone
they will want to
sacrifice you
for the sake of
heav'n
& the city
joe
woe joe's
city

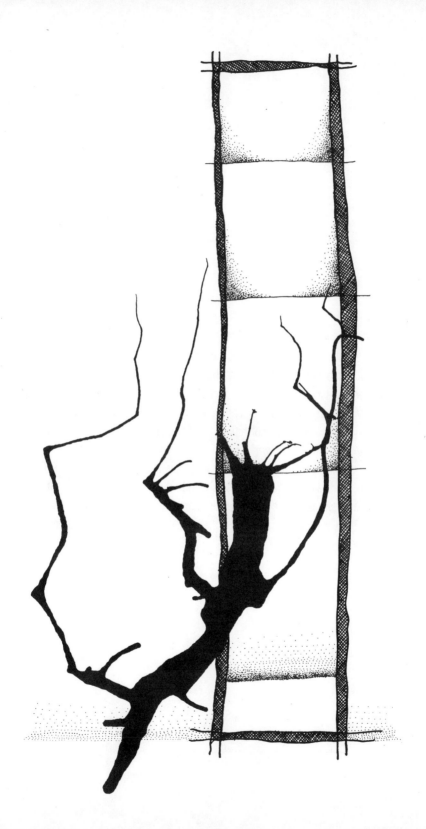

Rochelle Owens

Rochelle Owens, born April 2, 1936, is the award-winning author of many controversial and innovative plays and a pioneer in the experimental Off-Broadway movement. Her plays have been performed throughout the world and presented at festivals in Paris, Avignon, Berlin, Edinburgh and Rome. *Futz* was made into a feature-length film. She has published eight books of poetry, and two collections of plays, *Futz And What Came After*, and *The Karl Marx Play and Others*. She has edited *Spontaneous Combustion: Eight New American Plays*. A recipient of Guggenheim, C.A.P.S., National Endowment for the Arts. and the Yale School of Drama fellowships, she is on the board of directors for the Women's InterArt Center and now lives with her husband, the poet George Economou, in New York City.

POETRY

Not Be Essence That Cannot Be (1961)
Four Young Lady Poets (1962)
Salt and Core (1968)
I Am The Babe Of Joseph Stalin's Daughter (1972)
Poems From Joe's Garage (1973)
The Joe 82 Creation Poems (1974)
The Joe Chronicles Part 2 (1979)
Shemuel (1979)

PLAYS

Futz and What Came After (1968)
The Karl Marx Play and Others (1974)
The Widow and the Colonel (1977)

EDITOR

Spontaneous Combustion: Eight New American Plays (1972)

RECORDINGS

From A Shaman's Notebook (1968)
The Karl Marx Play (1975) (music by Galt MacDermot)
Totally Corrupt (1976)

FILM

Futz (1969)

PS3565 W57 S54
+Shemuel / Rochel+Owens, Rochelle.

0 00 02 0210084 8
MIDDLEBURY COLLEGE